QUEST FOR NEW
ANIMALS

written by David Alderton
illustrated by Studio Boni/Galante
and Ivan Stalio

CONTENTS

page

Finding New Animals 5

A Big Mistake 6

The Scope of the Sea 8

Mysteries of the Deep 10

Whales and Seals 12

Secrets of Frogs and Toads 14

Beware of the Dragon 16

Exciting Sightings *foldout* 18-21

Birds Back from the Brink *foldout* 22-24

Parrots' Paradise 25

New Birds 26

Animals in Hiding 28

Stealthy Hunters 30

Gathering the Clues 32

Do They Exist? 34

Amazing New Animal Facts 36

Glossary 37

Index 38

FINDING NEW ANIMALS

Every year, new creatures are being discovered on Earth. These can include quite large animals. Some amazing discoveries have been made over the past 100 years, and more finds, perhaps even a living dinosaur, may still await discovery.

White rhinoceros

White rhinoceroses are among the largest animals on Earth, so they should be easy enough to spot. Until 1900 however, they were believed to live only in southern Africa. Then a group was spotted over 3,000 kilometres away, proving that there are at least two sets of white rhinos in Africa.

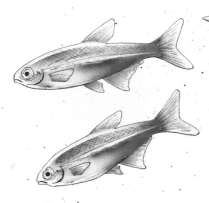

Neon tetras

In any shop that sells tropical fish, you will see neon tetras. They are now such popular aquarium fish that it is surprising to learn that they were not discovered until 1936. Neon tetras originally come from the river Amazon in South America.

Yemeni monitor lizard

Sometimes you don't even need to go out to wild places to find new animals today. This lizard was recognised as being unknown to science by a **zoologist** who saw it in a television programme in 1985.

A BIG MISTAKE

Once it was thought that all the world's big animals had been found, but we now know better. In order to be officially recognised, a new animal must be obtained – either dead or alive – so that it can be described in detail and **classified**. This means giving it a scientific name, and fitting it in with other animals, as part of the animal kingdom. The first new animal so classified is called the **type specimen**.

Baron Cuvier
This famous zoologist said in 1812 that he felt it was unlikely there were any large animals still undiscovered. He was wrong! Today, the search for new animals continues. It is called cryptozoology, from the Greek word *cryptos* meaning hidden, and *zoology*, the study of animals.

The tapir's nose can be used like a hand to pull down branches.

Malayan tapir
The existence of this tapir was confirmed by Diard, a pupil of Baron Cuvier's, just seven years after the Baron had suggested there were no more such animals to be found. Although there had been earlier reports of Malayan tapirs dating back to 1772, Cuvier himself had not believed them.

Giant panda

When the French explorer Père David was travelling through China in 1869 he saw a skin of a black and white animal which he assumed had been a bear.

It was, in fact, a giant panda which has since become one of the best-known animals in the world, although today it is highly **endangered** in the wild.

Okapi

Local African stories about forest donkeys led Sir Harry Johnston to search for these animals. He thought they might be a new type of zebra. Then he learnt that they had two hooves on each foot, unlike zebras and other members of the horse family, who have one. In 1901, when the okapi was discovered, it turned out to be a relative of the giraffe.

THE SCOPE OF THE SEA

Stories about sea monsters have been told for thousands of years. The world's oceans are some of the least-known areas on the planet, and they may well hide large creatures in their depths. Only if a body is washed up on a beach, or caught in the nets of a fishing boat can the existence of such animals be proved beyond doubt.

The kraken

This monster was believed to live in the seas off the coast of Norway. The kraken had many large arms, called tentacles, and was greatly feared. It was said to drag sailors overboard, and even destroy ships' masts with its powerful tentacles. Stories about the kraken may have been based on early sightings of giant squids.

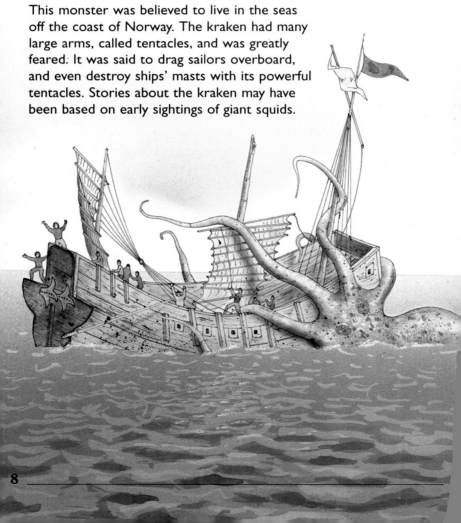

A MYSTERY IN A JAR

Scientists have recently tested samples from a huge, unidentified carcass which was washed ashore on a North American beach in 1896. The tests showed that the animal was a previously unknown giant octopus. Its body was known to have been 30 metres long.

Giant squid

The biggest giant squid ever found was eighteen metres long. Even bigger squids – perhaps ten times as large – may live in the world's oceans. Scars thought to be caused by their tentacles have been seen on dead whales.

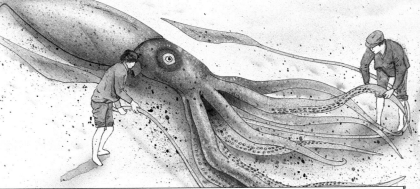

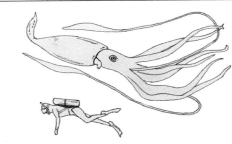

RELATIVE SIZE

Giant squids can be nine times as long as a large adult, and can have tentacles twice as long as their own bodies.

MYSTERIES OF THE DEEP

Recent deep sea exploration has meant that completely new types of fish have been found in the ocean depths. Some have proved to be living fossils, such as the goblin shark. Fossils of this shark were first found in the mid-1800s. Each had a strange protrusion, like a shovel, on the head above the jaws. Amazingly, a living example of a goblin shark was then caught in deep water close to the Japanese island of Yokohama in 1897. These sharks probably use their shovel-like projections to dig for worms on the seabed.

Coelacanth

Coelacanths were thought to have become **extinct** about 60 million years ago. Then in 1938, a trawler caught a strange fish which none of the fishermen on board could identify. This mysterious fish finally proved to be a coelacanth. It was fourteen years before another specimen was caught.

Megamouth shark

So called because of its huge mouth, the megamouth shark was discovered in 1976 as the result of a freak accident. One of these massive fish became caught up in a ship's anchor, and was hauled to the surface from a depth of about 150 metres. This megamouth shark was caught near the Hawaiian islands, off the west coast of America. Since then, others have been caught near Japan and Australia. The shark's mouth contains more than 100 rows of teeth which it uses to sieve tiny plankton.

RELATIVE SIZE

A megamouth shark is about three times the size of a large adult person, but only half the size of a great white shark. It is not dangerous to people.

Parasitic angler fish

One of a group of strange, ugly deep-sea fish, this particular angler fish is actually made up of three fish. The large female has two much smaller males permanently attached to her body. Part of the dorsal fin on the back of other angler fish has changed into a lure, looking rather like a fishing rod. This hangs down in front of the mouth and attracts small fish, which can then be snapped up.

WHALES AND SEALS

Although giant whales used to be heavily hunted by whaling fleets, smaller whales were not killed in such large quantities. This may explain why several types of smaller whales remained unknown until very recently. Unlike fish, however, these marine **mammals** must come up to the surface to breathe, so they are perhaps more likely to be seen.

Shepherd's beaked whale
In 1933, one of these whales became stranded on the western coast of North Island, New Zealand. Others have since been washed up on the coast of South America. They can grow to over six metres long.

Andrew's beaked whale
This whale was also first found on a New Zealand beach. Only eight specimens are known to scientists at present, with the first being identified in 1904.

They are thought to live in cool waters, and can grow to a length of at least four metres. They have distinctive beaks by which they are recognised.

Hawaiian monk seal

Living near the Hawaiian island of Laysan, this is the most recent seal to have been discovered, in 1905. Unfortunately, since then it has been heavily hunted for its fur, and probably no more than 1,000 remain alive. These seals sometimes look slightly greenish, because of microscopic **algae** growing on their fur.

Baja California porpoise

Found only in the Gulf of California, on America's western coast, this porpoise was unknown to science until 1950. It is the smallest known member of the whale family, growing to a size of a tall child and weighing less than a large dog!

13

SECRETS OF FROGS AND TOADS

Frogs and toads (**amphibians**) must live in damp surroundings because they breathe through their skins, which have to be kept moist. Many frogs and toads can be found in the world's rain forests, where it rains almost every day and the air is very humid.

Hairy frog

Living in the rain forests of West Africa, male hairy frogs grow folds of skin, which look rather like hairs, during the breeding period. The folds help these frogs to breathe more easily. Hairy frogs were first found in 1900.

Goliath frog

The rain forests of West Africa are also home to goliath frogs, the largest frogs in the world. Goliath frogs swim in fast flowing streams and were discovered in 1906.

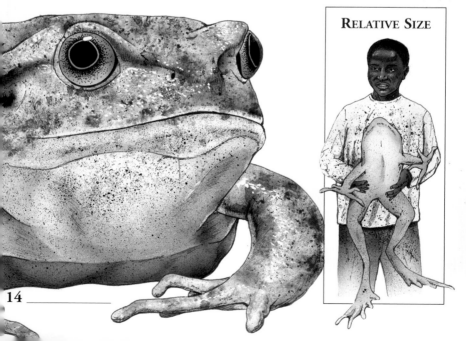

RELATIVE SIZE

Poison arrow frogs

No one knows how many different types of poison arrow frogs there are in Central and South America. This deadly one lives in Colombia, and was first recorded in 1973.

DEADLY DARTS

Darts tipped with the poison from some frogs are used by hunters to kill animals.

Mallorcan midwife toad

Fossilized remains of these toads were first discovered in 1977, on the island of Mallorca in the Mediterranean. Scientists believed they were extinct, but living examples were then found in 1980. These toads are very secretive, hiding in cracks in cliff faces. The males wrap the eggs around their back legs.

Gold toad

This is perhaps one of the most beautiful toads in the world, living in a valley in Panama, Central America. Gold toads first became known in 1929, but since then their numbers have fallen greatly, and they may soon become extinct.

BEWARE OF THE DRAGON

All reptiles are **cold-blooded**, so they are most common in tropical parts of the world. There they can remain active throughout the year, without having to **hibernate** over the winter. Some reptiles are confined to small islands. The Indonesian island of Komodo, for example, is home to the largest lizard in the world, the Komodo dragon, first heard of in Europe in 1912.

Weber's sailfin dragon

These lizards are found on two of the Moluccan islands, off the coast of southeast Asia. They grow to more than one metre long, and are so called because of the crest running down the centre of their back and tail. They were first discovered in 1911.

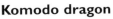

Komodo dragon

These huge **carnivorous** lizards can grow to over three metres long. They are fearsome hunters, eating pigs, goats and sometimes even people. Why such large lizards should have **evolved** on the small island of Komodo is unknown. They may have originally preyed on **pygmy** elephants which once lived there.

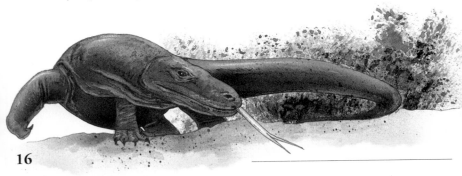

Pancake tortoise

Tortoises usually have hard, domed shells, but that of the pancake tortoise is very flat and soft. These particular tortoises, discovered in 1903, live in rocky areas of East Africa. They use their flattened shape to hide under stones and escape **predators**.

Light shells allow pancake tortoises to move very fast.

New Guinea crocodile

In 1908 a skull found in Papua New Guinea was proved to belong to the New Guinea crocodile. Up until then everyone had believed that the only crocodile living in the area was the Indo-Pacific crocodile. The New Guinea crocodile is smaller than its Indo-Pacific relative, only growing to four metres in length, and is also less aggressive.

HEAD OF A NEW GUINEA CROCODILE

The jaws of this crocodile are narrow, suggesting that it feeds mainly on fish.

EXCITING SIGHTINGS

Some animals are very secretive and hard to spot, which may make people think that they have died out. Those animals which live in trees and rarely, if ever, come down to the ground, can be particularly hard to see.

Tasmanian wolf
(Australia)
This is not really a wolf, but a **marsupial**, related to the kangaroo. Blamed for attacks on sheep, it was heavily hunted and was believed to be extinct by 1936. Recently, so many Tasmanian wolves have been seen and even photographed that zoologists are convinced they still survive in parts of Australia.

Leadbeater's possum (Australia)
Leadbeater's possum was once believed to have become extinct. But in 1961, two zoologists carrying out a survey in the state of Victoria found one in a tree. After more searching, they came across three others.

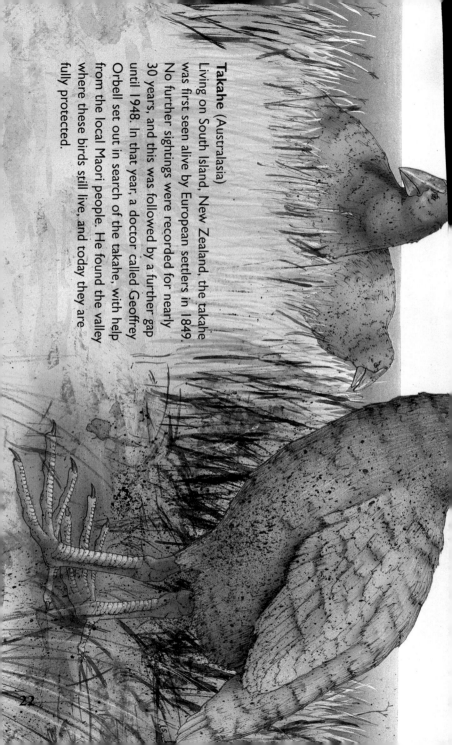

Takahe (Australasia)

Living on South Island, New Zealand, the takahe was first seen alive by European settlers in 1849. No further sightings were recorded for nearly 30 years, and this was followed by a further gap until 1948. In that year, a doctor called Geoffrey Orbell set out in search of the takahe, with help from the local Maori people. He found the valley where these birds still live, and today they are fully protected.

Celebes palm civet (Asia)
Looking rather like a dog, this mammal lives on the island of Sulawesi, which used to be called Celebes, in Indonesia. No sightings were made for over 30 years, and people believed it was extinct. Then one was seen and actually photographed in a palm tree in 1978.

Pygmy hog (Asia)
In 1971, a pygmy hog was caught in India, proving that it was not extinct, as scientists had thought.

Taipan (Australia)
This deadly snake was first seen in 1867, but it was not until 1923 that more were found.

BIRDS BACK FROM THE BRINK

Some birds have been rediscovered many years after they were believed to have become extinct. If the numbers of a specific bird or animal fall below a certain level however, they will not be able to breed properly. They are then almost certainly doomed to extinction.

Madagascan serpent eagle (Africa)

After the last sighting of this snake-eating eagle was made in 1930, it was not seen again until the summer of 1988. A dead Madagascan serpent eagle was then found two years later, and finally, in 1993, a live eagle was caught and photographed. Conservation work is now being carried out to help these rare eagles to survive.

Bermuda petrel (Americas)
This sea bird lives today on the small
Castle Harbour islands, close to the island
of Bermuda in the Atlantic Ocean. During
the 1620s this petrel was thought to have
been wiped out due to hunting by sailors
and black rats eating the birds' eggs.
Amazingly – more than 300 years later –
the Bermuda petrel is still alive.

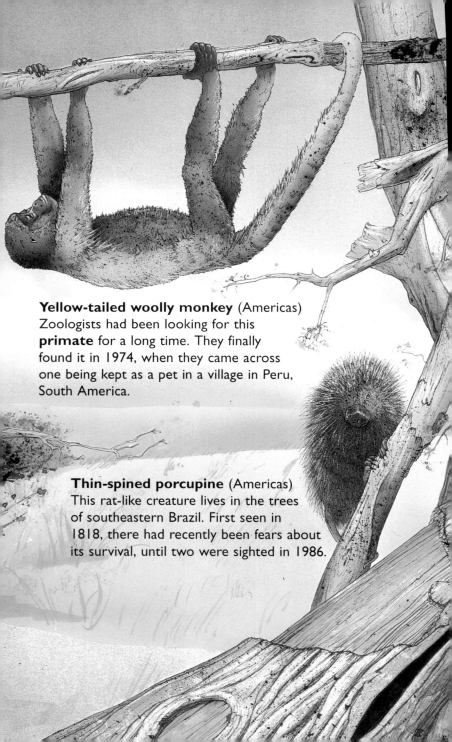

Yellow-tailed woolly monkey (Americas)
Zoologists had been looking for this
primate for a long time. They finally
found it in 1974, when they came across
one being kept as a pet in a village in Peru,
South America.

Thin-spined porcupine (Americas)
This rat-like creature lives in the trees
of southeastern Brazil. First seen in
1818, there had recently been fears about
its survival, until two were sighted in 1986.

PARROTS' PARADISE

There are 330 different types of parrots in the world today. In less than ten years, three new parrots have been found in South America alone, and there is still a strong chance that more new ones may be found.

El Oro conure

This parrot is named after the part of Ecuador in South America where it was first seen in 1980. The El Oro conure feeds on figs and other fruits in the treetops, and lives in flocks of between four and twelve birds.

Kawall's Amazon parrot

This mysterious parrot differs from other Amazon parrots by having a bald patch of skin round its lower bill. Until 1989, it was confused with the mealy Amazon, which it otherwise looks like.

Amazonian parrotlet

Parrotlets are among the smallest of all parrots, and they are hard to spot in the trees, because of their mainly green coloration. The Amazonian parrotlet was originally sighted in 1985. It lives in eastern Peru.

NEW BIRDS

Birds that live in remote parts of the world – even quite large birds – have remained unknown, although they may be familiar to local people. Reports of new birds come every year, and almost certainly there are more birds to be discovered, especially in the world's rain forest regions.

Congo peacock pheasant

While in Zaire, central Africa during 1913, an **ornithologist** called Dr Chapin saw a strange feather in a local headdress which he did not recognise. It came from a bird known locally as *mbulu*, but on his return to America, Dr Chapin still could not identify it. Many years later, in a Belgian museum, he saw two stuffed birds whose feathers matched the one in the headdress. He returned to Zaire in 1937, and found a living Congo peacock pheasant for the first time.

Mikado pheasant

Unknown tail feathers in another local headdress, on the island of Taiwan, near China, started the search for this Asian pheasant. Its magnificent tail feathers make up about half the mikado pheasant's total length. It was finally found in 1906.

Ribbon-tailed bird of paradise

Only the cock bird has these long, trailing tail feathers, which can be up to one metre long. They are about three-and-a-half times as long as the bird's body. This bird of paradise was unknown outside its Papua New Guinean homeland until 1936.

Long-whiskered owlet

This tiny owl's home is in the Andean mountains of northern Peru, where it was only discovered in 1976. The long-whiskered owlet is so called because of the whisker-like feathers on the sides of its face.

Imperial and Vo Quy's pheasants

Both these pheasants live in Vietnam, southeast Asia. The imperial was first found there in 1923, and has since been bred in **aviaries**. Vo Quy's pheasant remains more mysterious. It was originally seen in 1964. It is hoped that these pheasants will be bred at Vietnam's Hanoi Zoo.

Imperial

Vo Quy's

ANIMALS IN HIDING

Many large animals have been in existence for thousands of years but have only recently been discovered. This is often because they live in remote parts of the world. Some smaller animals have simply not been noticed.

Mountain gorilla

From the 1860s onwards, stories of monstrous apes were brought back by European explorers. But it was not until 1902 that scientific proof of their existence was finally obtained.

A mountain gorilla is larger than its lowland relatives. Sadly, this vegetarian ape is now endangered because it is being hunted.

Pygmy chimpanzee

A new type of chimpanzee was discovered in Africa during the 1920s. The pygmy chimpanzee is slimmer than the ordinary chimpanzee, with a blacker face. It lives in tropical forests, gathering fruit and other food in the trees, and uses its long arms to swing from branch to branch.

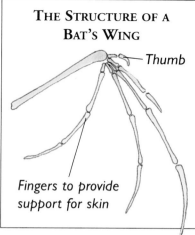

THE STRUCTURE OF A BAT'S WING

Thumb

Fingers to provide support for skin

Kitti's hog-nosed bat

This bat is one of the world's smallest mammals. It is no bigger than a bumblebee, with a nose which looks like the snout of a pig! These bats were first found in a cave in Thailand, southeast Asia, in 1973.

Giant forest hog

Living in the dense rain forest areas of Africa, this giant hog is the largest pig in the world. It stands nearly a metre tall at the shoulder, and can be over two metres long. The existence of the giant forest hog was confirmed in 1904.

Donkey pig

The real name of this wild pig is the chacoan peccary. Local people call it the donkey pig because of the shape of its ears. It was thought to have died out during the last ice age, over 10,000 years ago. But in 1974 it was discovered that the chacoan peccary had actually survived.

STEALTHY HUNTERS

Quiet and secretive by nature, wild cats are never easy to spot. Most wild cats are **nocturnal**, hunting at night, which means they are less likely to be seen. Tracks, and signs of their kills, are the best clues to their presence in an area. During the 1980s, several new cats were found.

King cheetah
Instead of spots, the king cheetah's coat is marked with black stripes. It was first reported in 1926, from the African country of Zimbabwe. It was not until the 1980s that the king cheetah was proved to be a rare tabby form of the ordinary cheetah.

Iriomote cat
The Iriomote cat was unknown until 1967, and is very rare indeed. It is named after the island of Iriomote, to the south of Japan, where it lives. Only about 100 of these cats live on the island, and they are sometimes caught and eaten by local people.

Tshushima cat

This cat lives on the island of Tshushima, between Japan and South Korea. It is thought that less than 100 of these cats live there. The Tshushima cat was first discovered in 1988, but little is known about its habits so far.

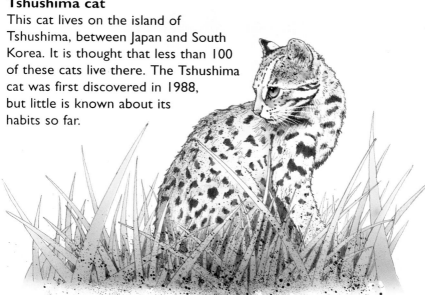

Onza

Back in the early 1500s, the first Spanish explorers wrote about a large, long-legged wild cat which lived in Mexico. It wasn't until 1986 that the existence of the onza was at last confirmed. These cats hunt deer, and probably other large animals.

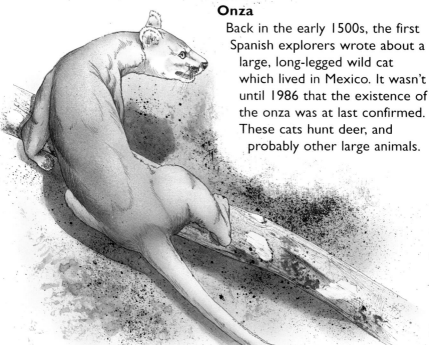

GATHERING THE CLUES

Finding new animals is not just a matter of luck. Listening to people talking about their local wildlife can give clues. Studying **hunting trophies**, carvings and paintings for evidence of unknown animals are all useful methods of locating new species. These factors helped to find the **herbivorous** animals on this page.

Vu Quang ox

In 1992, zoologists working in Vietnam in southeast Asia, saw some unusual horns in the homes of local hunters. Those horns came from the Vu Quang ox, which may be a relative of the cow and the antelope.

Kouprey

This ox, also from Asia, may be truly wild, or it may be a **domesticated** animal that has gone back to the wild. Carvings of the kouprey are known to date back over 800 years, but its existence was only officially confirmed in 1937.

Mountain buffalo

This tiny buffalo lives in the mountainous forest on the large island of Sulawesi, off the southeast coast of Asia. It is about as high as an adult's shoulder, and was first recorded in 1910.

Mountain nyala

The home of this large antelope is high up in the Sahatu mountains of Ethiopia, in the northeast of Africa. There it lives and grazes on the flat areas called plateaus. It too was discovered in 1910.

BAMBOO LEMUR

The only place this lemur is found is on the island of Madagascar, off the southeastern coast of Africa. Golden bamboo lemurs were seen for the first time in 1985. They are so called because they feed only on bamboo. Another, larger type of bamboo lemur, thought to have become extinct in the early 1900s, was rediscovered on Madagascar in 1972.

DO THEY EXIST?

The search goes on for mysterious creatures that may live on our planet. So far we have no proof that any of the animals shown here do actually exist, but each one is claimed to have been seen a number of times. One of the most likely to be found in the future is probably the Congo swamp monster, which may be a living **sauropod**-type of dinosaur. It is said to live in water, using its long neck to feed on the hard rain forest chocolate fruits which grow along the riverbanks.

Congo swamp monster

This animal has been reported in a part of Africa which has hardly changed at all since dinosaurs died out, about 65 million years ago.

It is called *mokele-mbembe* by the local people, who say it is reddish in colour and up to nine metres in length.

Bigfoot in North America

This massive creature might prove to be a large ape, which lives in small family groups like gorillas. The Indian people of the heavily forested region it is believed to inhabit call it *sasquatch*. Over 10,000 sightings have been recorded, and there is also a film which claims to show a living bigfoot.

FOOTPRINTS

Further evidence of bigfoot's existence is based on footprints

Supposed bigfoot footprint   *Human footprint*

The Loch Ness monster

Britain's most famous mysterious animal is said to live in Scotland's Loch Ness, a large and very deep lake. Sightings of creatures like sea serpents have been made over hundreds of years, but there is little real evidence of them.

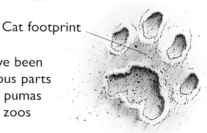

Cat footprint

Mysterious cats

For the past twenty years, there have been reports of large wild cats from various parts of Britain. Some people believe that pumas or panthers that have escaped from zoos are now breeding in the wild.

AMAZING NEW ANIMAL FACTS

- **Mystery swallow** In 1984, the body of an unknown swallow was found on an island in the Middle East. It has become known as the Red Sea cliff swallow. No similar swallows have ever been recorded.

- **The aggressive ape** Although no apes are believed to live in South America, a strange ape-like creature was once photographed there. This was in 1920, close to the border between Colombia and Venezuela. The animal was shot dead as it was about to attack a group of scientists.

- **A rare find in a squashed snake** In 1992, when Graham Armstrong examined a snake that had been run over on a road close to the town of Burra, South Australia, he recognised this reptile's last meal. It had been a pygmy blue-tongued skink, thought to have been extinct since 1959. Searching the area nearby, he then rediscovered a group of these lizards. Some are now being bred at Adelaide Zoo.

- **Mystery giant Asian elephants** Tall elephants with large domed swellings on their foreheads were reported from a remote part of western Nepal in 1992. They may be a new type of elephant, possibly the living descendants of an extinct form called *Stegodon*.

- **Millions of insects** Zoologists think that there could be as many as 50 million different invertebrates living in the world's rain forest areas. This would mean that a huge number still await discovery.

- **A predicted discovery** The famous naturalist Charles Darwin predicted the existence of a butterfly or moth with a very large tongue. No one believed him at the time, but in 1903 – over forty years after Darwin suggested the idea – the Madagascan long-tongued hawk moth was finally found.

GLOSSARY

Algae Tiny plants that live in or near water.

Amphibian An animal that can live on land but must return to water to breed.

Aviary A place for keeping birds.

Carnivore An animal that only eats meat.

Classified An animal that has been recorded and given a scientific name.

Cold-blooded An animal whose body temperature changes with the temperature of its surroundings.

Domesticate To make an animal able to live with people.

Endangered When a species of animal is in danger of dying out completely.

Evolve To change gradually over many years and adapt to new conditions.

Extinct When an animal has died out and no longer exists.

Herbivore An animal that feeds on grass and plants.

Hibernate To go into a long sleep during the winter.

Hunting trophy The head or skin of an animal that has been mounted on a wall as a decoration.

Mammal An animal that is fed, when young, on milk from its mother's body.

Marsupial An animal that carries its young in a pouch.

Nocturnal Happening or active at night.

Ornithologist A scientist who studies birds.

Predator An animal that lives by killing and eating other animals.

Primate A member of a group of mammals that includes humans and monkeys.

Pygmy A species of animal that is smaller than usual.

Sauropod A plant-eating dinosaur with a long neck and tail.

Type specimen The first example from which all animals of the same kind are described.

Zoologist A scientist who studies the behaviour and habitats of animals.

INDEX *(Entries in **bold** refer to an illustration)*

A — *pages*

Amazonian parrotlet 25
Andrew's beaked whale 12
angler fish 11

B

Baja California porpoise 13
bamboo lemur 33
Bermuda petrel 23
bigfoot 35

C

Celebes palm civet 19
chacoan peccary 29
coelacanth 10
Congo peacock pheasant 26
Congo swamp monster 34
cryptozoology 6

E

El Oro conure 25

F

fossils 10, 15

G

giant forest hog 29
giant panda 7
giant squid 9
goblin shark 10
gold toad 15
goliath frog 14

H

hairy frog 14
Hawaiian monk seal 13

I — *pages*

imperial pheasant 27
Iriomote cat 30

K

Kawall's Amazon parrot 25
king cheetah 30
Kitti's hog-nosed bat 29
Komodo dragon 16
kouprey 32
kraken 8

L

Leadbeater's possum 21
Loch Ness monster 35
long-whiskered owlet 27

M

Madagascan serpent eagle 24
Malayan tapir 6
Mallorcan midwife toad 15
megamouth shark 11
mikado pheasant 26
mountain buffalo 33
mountain gorilla 28
mountain nyala 33

N

neon tetra 5
New Guinea crocodile 17

O

okapi 7
onza 31